Also by Michael Potts

Fiction

End of Summer
Unpardonable Sin
Obedience
Slipknot and Other Dark Tales

Poetry

From Field to Thicket
Hiding from the Reaper and Other Horror Poems

Nonfiction

*Aerobics for the Mind: Practical Exercises in Philosophy that
Anybody can Do*

Slipknot and Other Dark Poems

Michael Potts

Published by Heartsblood Press, 2021.

SLIPKNOT AND OTHER DARK POEMS

First edition. September 27, 2021.

Copyright © 2021 Michael Potts.

ISBN: 979-8201011741

Written by Michael Potts.

Also by Michael Potts

Death Rattle and Other Dark Tales
Slipknot and Other Dark Poems

Watch for more at www.michael-potts.com.

Table of Contents

What I Shall Become

I was four when the house
burned, a short in a stove wire
turning my first home

into ash. White smoke
rose into indefinite sky,
dispersed like a last breath.

Sometimes I feel myself
fading, steam from a boiling
kettle never reaching

the ceiling. The world
dims, a flashlight
with failing power,

my heart a car battery
in cold weather that can't
start the engine. Today,

there's a highway built over
the ashes of my childhood.
I walk on dust I will become.

What Mist Hides

Heavy rain-mist hides evergreens
behind a white-sheath fog. Cold
wind whips my hair, slips under
my coat, grips. Inside, a nurse
takes vitals, attends the needs
of a body that in two weeks will be
ashes and fragments of bone. *You
can come in now*. I do, thaw
in the room's warmth, stroke
the remains of your hair. You look
stronger than yesterday—time
to pray again for a miracle—
but your body lies waiting
for Death to steal you away.
You smile, we hug, feel
breath bless. I want to keep life
inside, stop its leaking, hold back
the cold clasp of Death's hand—
but cancer-racked, you're ready.
Through tear-mist I tell myself
I'll be able to bear the news when
it comes. I lie beside you, clasp
your waist. Your hand grasps mine,
shifts it to the hollow over your heart.
The strong thumps lie to me.
You press down my hand
as if I could stop your soul
from going—and for a moment
we both believe, Now I must
leave for the airport, hoping.

Yet in eight days you go away
to hide behind mist, to walk
beneath timeless trees.

Old Photo

A woman rests serene in an oval frame.
Long auburn hair hangs,
two strands draped over her right
shoulder, an oversized thickness
of braided hair drooping her left.
Loose folds of a white dress hide
her torso. Her pupils—fixed.
Does she stare and think of a lost
lover? Or is she dead, propped
for a photo, mouth frozen
in an enigmatic frown, lips
sewn shut, silent for a final pose.

At the Grave

A thin film of ice forms on the pond
as I walk over hay whitened by frost.
Summer's long fled to the southern
hemisphere, and the oaks and maples
spit out the last of their leaves
months ago. White steam rises
over cold water, disappearing
before reaching the tops of tall oaks.

Walking away from the pond, I find
my family cemetery, the place I lay
my wife to rest five years ago.
And now, in the dead of February,
stepping over brown hay that hides
dirt covering underneath decay,
I strip off my coat, lie on frozen
ground to rest in peace. Before
I close my eyes, a patch of green

daffodil shoots appear around my wife's
grave. How? Planted by whom? I must wait
for them to bloom. Crawling to my coat,
I slip it on, stand, savoring the moment
of new-found life. Wrapping myself
in the warmth of winter clothes,
I walk home, ready to return tomorrow.

Checking Out

Here lie bare bones,
carved stones above our skulls.
We lie side by side,
rest in matching caskets
covered with identical vaults,
two added to the hundred billion
plus, part of the mortal crowd.
We cow the living to terror –
they dread our fate, hearts
thumping to us and our kind.
The thought of us haunts them
into drink, drugs, wealth, sex,
and shop until they drop by,
to join us – except there's no *us*
here. We're elsewhere, souls
spying on our remains,
the longing for our bodies
a gnawing hunger as we
await their fated return.

Seizing Ownership: An Acrostic

Into my heart a harbinger
Nestles, her sing-song voice
Filling me with longing.
Each day her charms grow,
Seeding my mind, trying
To trap. She has ESP
And knows about my death-obsession.
Tina tells of her near-death experience
In a hospital ER, her heart stopping
Owing to a blood clot in her lungs;
Now she's tugging me into herself.

On her cue I know I am in love,
Promising her my life, not knowing
Pain would prick us past the time we wed.
Riding high after our honeymoon,
Each day her jealousy grows, darkens,
Stopping my life with overbearing will,
Stepping on freedom, keeping me
Inside except for work.
Others think our life to be idyllic,
Not hearing nightly shouts and screams.

Penetrating inside, she gains dominion
Over my will, my very being,
Smothering any trace of autonomy,
Scraping every fleck of self-
Esteem until none remains, my
Soul her prisoner, with any leftover

Scraps of my spirit empty of
Identity, a wholly owned subsidiary
Of her—she who wins –
Now no *I* remains; only *she*.

Mirror

Branches rock with the ebb and flow
of wind. A man walks by the lake, his boots
stomping through mud and slush. Limestone
outcroppings jut out over water. He spreads
a blanket, sits and watches fish splash, fins
flipping drops toward the sun, sparking
and dimming like fireflies. They fall back
to a polished surface where mirrored trees
spread out upside down. He imagines walking
on the lake into that world, climbing a tree
from tip to trunk until he's upside down.
Then he lets go, flying through space.

Yesterday, he lost his wife and job. In mid-
affair, she left, moved away with her lover.
Folks say that sometimes you regress, go
back where you're stuck, your life turned upside
down. The man considers this as he stoops over
a ledge, staring at smooth limestone islets jutting
from the surface fifty feet below. The man
rises, stands, takes a step, and watches
his reflection grow larger as he falls.

Steel Drum

The woman burns the dead man's sheets
in a rusty steel drum full of holes. Blackened
fabric flakes fly into a gray sky. The sun
begins to set, but the fire burns—yellow,
orange, red—finishing the final remnants
of her dead husband she'd wrapped inside—
his skull, now black, grinning a greeting.

Potter's Field

The old man's cane slips on a rock—
he starts to slide but breaks his fall.
Stumbling ahead, tracks guide him
toward the liquor store. But he's lost

track of time—the moon descends
below cedar branches. It's dark
and the man's tired, so he lies down,
cane by his side, a cross tie

his pillow. Too late he hears
the whistle and he sits up—
his fatal mistake—a final
scream, obliterated face,

body carved into head,
trunk, two severed legs—
worse, he'll rest unmissed,
unmourned, in the Potter's Field.

Ice Cold

The creek was deep,
the bank steep
and slick with mud,

brown clay, the kind
that causes shovels to stick
when people dig graves.

God, it must have been
ninety that day.
The boy was four-
years-old and hot
from running

with his dog, Jack,
who licked him until
the boy played dead
and the dog stood guard.

All the boy wanted
was cool water.

Last week, he'd dipped
his feet into ice-cold relief
while Mama and Daddy
fished, but today,

Mama wasn't watching
and Daddy wasn't home

when the boy wandered
into his short obituary.

It's Going to Happen

In the mirror
gray hairs
invade brown.

I turn away
to forget

until lunch when
my knees pop
like an old man's.

I take a walk,
to forget

until bedtime when
my heart
skips three beats.

Falling asleep,
I dream

of childhood,
my aging dog
sick in his pen,

my rifle primed
for a fatal shot.

Last Breath

Granddaddy burned the sheets
after Uncle Irwin died.
Now I lie in that same bed,
new sheets, new spread
protecting me from cold
and, I hope, more. I was here

that day, the dead man's bare
chest white, still as windless
night. *Where does the last breath
go after death?* I wondered

and ask again as a quarter-moon
puts out pale light. I shut my eyes,
turn on my left side, hear my heartbeat
magnified through the mattress
which quickens when a puff of air
lifts my hair, the remains of a final,
corpse-cold, exhalation.

Role Playing

We play Dungeons and Dragons
by candlelight, teenagers, barely
in high school, oblivious to the dying

day outside. Hours pass away
to midnight, our minds lost
in the dungeon, as we become

our characters: Erik, fighter,
Clovis, cleric, Edward, thief—
courses charted by the dungeon

master on a sheet of notebook paper.
We reach a pot of gold
Where goblins attack.

Clovis is killed. We stop the game
to refill our Cokes. A scream, not
of the dungeon, shrieks us clean

out of our imaginations. Shaking
with real fear, we call it
a night, return to our homes.

The next morning, I read
the paper, find, tucked away
on page seven, a story of a man

killed by a train round midnight,

under the influence of alcohol.
I tell the group the next day.

We sit in silence, knowing that
the game will never be the same.
We ponder the real pain which drove

a man to drink, his intoxicated eyes
staring at death's bright eye
glaring, our imaginations

stripped away by the rawness
of reality which arrived
too soon.

Overheard

The surgeons cross the border of skin, muscle, and blood
into my belly where a tumor rests, a coiled snake
sunning in body heat, waiting to be disturbed
and strike out life from my body. Now I hear,
as I wake from an anesthesia fog, doctors talking:

Malignancy.
Multiple metastasises.

Buffeted by word-blows, I'm cursed from being
well-read in medicine. A doctor notices
my tachycardic heart, and penning a note
on my chart, tells me, *The surgery's over, relax,*
we'll run more tests later. When? I ask.
Later... Don't worry now. Lie still and get some rest.

As I'm wheeled into my room, I think of roses resting
in a bed, oblivious to their inescapable wilting, the sound
of wind pushing their petals into a wordless dance.

A Win at Chess

I glide the bishop across the board,
slide it along the white diagonal
to take Bob's black rook. He gasps,
cheeks redden into twin apples,
hands rise, covering his face. Then
his right hand unpeels from his head,
moves toward the king, his fingers
flicking it to the board, resigning.

Bob shakes my hand, dejected,
and slinks away, shoulders drooping,
gray hair and white dress shirt
disappearing through the side door.
While I don't know Bob except
as a chess rival, I almost regret
winning. Next month,

at another tournament, Bob's not
on the players' list. I question the director,
who tells me Bob died the night
of the last tournament of a shotgun wound
to the head, self-inflicted.

Wilting

I pluck white and yellow daffodils,
cradle them in my arms, place them
in a water-filled vase, arranging
a bouquet that graces my table
for days before colors fade,
the blooms wilting and sagging.

In the photo on my fireplace mantle,
I'm two, the freshness of my face
shining, certain of better days ahead.
Today, I can't look for long, my arthritic
neck in agony, legs bending, skin
sagging—at eighty-eight, it won't be
long before my body rests in earth.

Time for a fresh bouquet—I take
out the rotting flowers, wrapped
in a paper shroud, carry them
to my garden and bury them.

Bad Neighbor

For nine months we were
neighbors, our homes close

though we never visited
though we were brothers

of two eggs
of two sperm
in two wombs.

On Christmas day I led the way;
you followed, and we both
swallowed our first life-puffs.

We cried.
Two hours passed.
You died.

For years you haunted
me with fears of death,
that skull-faced
graceless monster
who took you.

Years later I read
your death certificate—
bilateral pulmonary edema,
severe; erythroblastosis.

How did our blood mix
through divided walls?
Was I a fetal vampire,
sucking your lifesblood,
turning your lungs
into a sponge-bath of death?

Was your revenge this
haunting, a fear of joining
you beneath cold earth?

Beating Death

I lie on my side underneath a large oak.
Standing stones surround me like approaching
Death. But he won't get here today, to this place
of graves. I tell him he wouldn't steal me away
early, like my twin brother, torn from life
two hours after birth, blood mucking his lungs
until he drowned.

Once is enough, Dark Angel.
I lurk in your territory, waiting to break
your skinny hand. I know one day you'll take me,
but not yet, not until I'm old with hair white
as your bleached bones. Then my brother and I
will rise, and in the light of day that's never night
we'll play over your grave. I'll dance to the sounds
of your xylophone ribs, my brother beating out
a rhythm with your arm-bone sticks, as we crush
your devil-bones to dust.

It Comes in Twos

The first time
the boy thought deeply
about death,
he was six.
He'd seen
a dead rabbit
beside the highway,
and wondered
what would happen
if he himself
were hit.

When he turned eight,
his great-grandfather lay,
wearing a black suit
and tie, in a steel casket
at Miller's Funeral Home.
The dead man's lips
turned up in a smirk.

At ten
his parents drove
past a wreck.
The boy looked out
the rear window
of their Chevy
at a bloody sheet
and felt a chill.

He was twelve,
hunting quail,
the day his dad
collapsed,
turned pale
as paper,
the eyes
rolling back.

Two weeks later,
the boy masturbated
for the first time.

Sno-Cone Truck

The sno-cone truck plays an old cabaret tune,
but the kids don't know that as they rush,
pockets stuffed with change, to buy a grape
or cherry. It's nice, I think, and almost run outside
to buy the icy drink—but opening the door,
my mind shrinks into memory, back fifteen years,

at my parents' place for a year to save money
for a Master's degree, walking my childhood
lawn, hearing the distant song of a sno-cone
truck. I didn't buy anything, no cash in hand
or pocket—and didn't care—my eyes were fixed
next door on Trent Delgado's house. Trent,

neighbor for nineteen years, Daddy's fishing
buddy, his wife Amy Mama's companion
in shopping and sewing and gossip. Not my
friends but familiar faces and voices.
But that summer Amy was in her house

somewhere, cancer feeding on her insides, eating
her body to death. Summer's heavy air stank
of stalking death. The sno-cone truck's song
became a dirge — every day at three o'clock
it would come. I'd dread its arrival,
its reminder, now that years fly

like swift blackbirds, I hate the tones
of sno-cone trucks, the thought

of their cold cargo chilly as the grave,
their happy child's music cancer to my ears.

Hell if I Know What This Has to Do with the Ethical Treatment of Animals

If I think of the dry, cracked clay of my life,
I'll fall into a crack,
clutch the sides, feel fingernails splitting,
smell the rot of leaves, the bitter leavings
of earthworms seeping into my mouth,
hear the grate of knees
against rough earth in the rich,
palpable dark, thick like paste,
or like the rotten peanut I found
in my box of Cracker Jacks
at Uncle Bill Stark's in Nashville
when I was six.

But I'm not falling into a crack.
One day at my grandparents,
in their front yard,
I opened the door
of an ancient refrigerator,
and locked myself in,
found just in time,
I had already metempsychosed
into another life
and been reborn as a serpent.

Goodness gracious sakes alive!
was Granny's commentary
on my near-death experience,
that sharp aroma of reality.

I felt relieved, great,
like a full-bellied vulture,
like I'd eaten a dead cow
in three minutes flat.
Tomorrow, I'll eat death.

But today, I'm busy
pulling the fur off a rabbit,
planning on eating

wild meat for dinner
and laughing.

Manifestum est, tempus, et aeternitatem non esse idem.

My calico cat said that
after a day of smoking catnip,

just before a crack
opened in the earth
and she fell in.

Shop 'Till You Drop

Dark leaves crackle beneath rain
drops striking blows of fate.
Distant crows cackle and wait,
their claws clinching power
lines. One crow caws, flies
toward a gray running form,
clutches and carries a rabbit.

In stores, humans scamper on Black
Friday, hop from shop to shop.
They fail to see the crows
hover over their heads who wait
for their inevitable prey.

Inviting Death to Dinner

Whenever I consider
the dry clay of my life,
I fall into a crack,
clutch the sides,
fingernails splitting,
odor of leaf-rot,
bitter leavings
of earthworms
seeping into my mouth.
My knee joints grate
against rough earth
in the rich, palpable dark,
the taste of death
thickening like paste.

But I'm not falling
into a crack. One day
at my grandparents,
in their front yard,
I opened the door
to an ancient refrigerator,
and locked myself in,
found just in time.

Lordy, Lordy, Lordy!
was Granny's commentary
on my near-death experience
as the sharp tang of lifesaving air
rushed into my lungs.

I felt relieved, great,
like a full-bellied vulture,
like I'd eaten a dead hog
in three minutes flat.

Tomorrow I'll eat death,
treat myself to tasty bones.

Valley of the Shadow

I'm sitting
in my rocking chair
grading papers
for a philosophy class:
uneventful routine
bores the evening,
my eyes open and close
in semi-sleep, and thoughts
begin to fly away from order.

Fear of death hits me
like a solid shadow,
a steam locomotive,
its smokestack seething in ghost-blow
on a full-moon night, wheels
rolling the obese train
along squeaking tracks as I lay
tied to the tracks:
a rope burns my bound wrists
and ankles, as the cool-fingers-air
of night touches my naked chest
nesting my heart which is jolting
and jumping be-bop be-bop,
a modern jazz dirge cause it's scared,
just waitin' for that train to come.

My mind returns to grading papers.
I notice that I'm rocking fast. Looks
like a long night.

Out of Winter's Ruins

Black birds like dots escape the northern sky
on their way to warmer lands below.
Ice coats granite with a sun-drenched glaze;
a winter's death grip wants nothing to thrive.
Off the pond-fog's smoky inferno,
Cold-corpse wind shifts gray-white haze
that slides until it strikes a lone green blade,
of dandelion prepared, eager to grow
come March into yellow bloom ablaze.
From pallid ruins a vital spirit flows—
the scythe of death the shield of life delays.

Full Lunar Eclipse, Stones River National Battlefield

I walk on the gray grass of a February field.
The ghosts of dead blades glow white
in the light of the rising moon. Now it's ten,
time for a full lunar eclipse, the world
darkening, the whiteness of the full moon
bloodying into red, ground filling
with the spent lives of soldiers' spirits,
men cut in half by cannonballs or stopped,
mid-stride, by lead. Shadows shift
and a torso rises. His dark hand grips
a rifle. He drops it, raises his arms,
flings them in the air before he sinks back
into the red clay, as if he recognized,
too late, the futility of it all.

Nihilism

Despair darker than the blankness
of death haunts the man at two a.m.,
the time he thinks about his extinction,
consciousness wiped out like a smudge
of dirt by a cloth. Sitting up, throat
tightening, he glances at the clock
by his bed, red letters passing time,
marking dead moments, the present's
constant killing by the past. The man

gasps air that suddenly seems thin,
grasps at meaning that hangs on a cliff's
edge, but it falls as he lunges, disappears
as if never existing at all.

The Dry Well

When I haul up the rotten rope
from the old dry well of time,
the rope breaks, the rusted pail
of my body clanging to the dry
bottom, where dust, life evaporated
of meaning, leaves me lying
on my side, alone, with only
rusty hope that my body will rise
again whole, a pail filled
with the fresh cold water of eternity.

Scallop Shell

A clump of brown seaweed from the morning tide
covers a scallop. I free the shell. It polished surface
glistens. The same sun beats my bare back with heat,
its rays swarm through sunblock, broils my skin
from brown to red. Waves climb onto the gray-sand
shore, lifting leavings of life, shells black and white,
blue, or tinged with pink. Standing up, I watch
water roll, see the sea as a womb, an amniotic sac
baptizing life with food and drink. I lift up

the scallop shell, empty of by the animal
inside. It was once alive, mouth opening
to the ocean to feed until a predator came,
split the shell, ate soft flesh until filled.
The beach received the remains I lift and hold
in my hand. Pain stabs my palm; I drop
the shell, its serrated edge sharp as a saw,
find a jagged cut. Instinct moves hand to mouth,
and I taste the salt of the womb.

Losing Feeling

I look out my window
through half-open blinds,
the sky an upside down
bowl of gray resting
on earth. I've just turned
forty-four, the double-digit
of middle age, trying not
to think of dying, trying
to stay alive, to live a life
outside weekends, dredging out
meaningless weekdays, Mondays
coming too fast, Tuesdays,
Wednesdays, Thursdays, Fridays
dragging as I write another
report, adding and subtracting
to un-tax the rich. Life's
a bitch; I'm a spore thrown
down a gray slope onto boring
existence, nothing more.
Seconds flow slow on workdays,
but weeks, months, years
fly fast like swift clouds.

What to do? Have sex with a
woman on my den floor so I may
feel something, any sensation better
than nothing, even pain will do—
hard drugs, a few martinis, mixed
with a dominitrix—or else

will I find some chick
at a bar, where we click,
fall head over heels
into marriage, divorce, death?

Another day of working late.
It's Friday. The bars stay open
until 2 A.M. Outside, the sky
thickens with dark, a bowl
blackening to night.

Message to my Heart

You're an expert on giving false
hope—I feel your life-throbs
lie to me, telling me I shall live
forever. At night, you say
again, again, "Alive, alive,
alive," and I'm trying to be
grateful for your help.

But there's a rub, and you
know it. Eventually you'll just give
up. I can see it now: I'm minding
my own business mowing the lawn,
and all of sudden you just decide
to skip out and quit on me. "Alive,
alive—OOPS—I think I'll STOP!"

Who the hell is going to finish
mowing the lawn now? But it could be
even worse: in the throes of passion
with my wife you decide that the climax
of my life should take place, my limp
body plopping down on her breasts.
You don't have my permission

to stop then—as if I have any say
in the matter. Planned obsolescence is fine
for Fords, Pentiums, leisure suits, door hinges,
biodegradable cups, and gall bladders—
but for you? Don't get me wrong. I appreciate

what you do. We've put up with one another
for 40 years. Do me a favor, will ya? Stick around

a while. Forever would be nice. I'd miss
hearing your soothing voice through my pillow
at night whispering sweet somethings
in my ear. I know you're gonna screw me
in the end. But, as folks say, "Such is life."
I'll be a good sport and share a beer with you.

The Web of Belief

I fell in love the moment you told me
about your death, the slowing of your heart
to a standstill, your vision of hell
and heaven with Jesus standing in the light.
You said I was the only one who knew
about your near-death experience, and that
trust bound us as links binding a chain.

We talked of Moody's book, *Life after Life,*
of our own lives having Asperger's
Syndrome, bullied by our peers
at school, my obsession over death,
yours over music, listening to Sting,
his existential message striking you
to contemplate what lesser people missed.

We're twins, you said, and I believed the lie
that drew my feelings to betray my wife
and wound my marriage to a spider's web.
You never died the day you claimed you did,
never saw hell nor heaven nor Jesus Christ,
your words, a tapestry devoid of truth,
you weaved to hide your nothingness inside.

Mad Dash

On the road at last, after four hour's sleep,
after teaching morning classes–*what a sun!*
What breezes this May afternoon! driving
to Chapel Hill, 401 North, 55 North.
Must eat lunch, stop at McDonald's
in Lillington, Big Mac meal,
fast! fast! Must eat fast! Out–
goddamned traffic! Slow asses!
Is she in surgery? She must be by now,
is she OK–pleaseGodletherbeOK.

I stop at Winn-Dixie and question the cut flowers,
What flowers would be appropriate? Roses?
After all, she's just a friend, isn't she, she must be,
I'm married, she's married, notalover,
Jesus don't let me think this way today,
but I buy a dozen daisies, pretty enough,
already roses. I-40, exit Hwy. 54: *The University*
of North Carolina at Chapel Hill and I find
the hospital, its buildings stalwart and respectable,
and there's actually a place to park.

I'm here to see Linda Allen. "Room 514," I'm told.

Elevator, 5th floor, *heartpoundingIentertheroom*–
but she's still in recovery. Pacing, I write a poem
in my head–write without paper the confession
I'm not ready to make.

Slipknot

Lights out, Lynn lies
by the dying embers
in her fireplace,
watching the red glow
of burnt fruit wood
before it turns black,

and remembering a boy
from college twenty
years before, Dave,
who called her one night
to ask her out. Dave—
the science nerd
who dared to phone Lynn,
a cheerleader and president
of the Delta Phi Delta sorority.

She didn't tell him *No*
at first but said she'd call him
back. She invited her
sorority sisters, carried
the phone into her bathroom,
dialed Dave's number,
told him *Dave, I have
a message for you,*
set the phone on the toilet
and flushed, laughing
with her friends.

Now, as the fire flickers
into darkness, Lynn turns on
the light, calls directory assistance.
Time for an apology, time
to ease her burning conscience.
She hears a phone ring
a thousand miles away,
but Dave doesn't hear a thing.

Ten minutes before she called,
he remembered Lynn
and that phone call to his dorm,
the sound of her toilet
being flushed, his roommate's
laughter. He looked
over the filthy floor
of his apartment
and remembered quitting
college, working odd jobs,
three marriages and divorces.

He carried a kitchen chair
to the bathroom, tied a rope
to the light fixture, wrapped it
snug around his neck,
and tied a knot. As he fell,
in the apartment above him
the last sound he heard
was a toilet's flush.

Strays

Splattered acid—
a cancer-eaten brain.

Her stray memories
come and go:

bee sting
by the barn door
at four;

at six,
a pony ride
in Aunt Fanny's field;

now she's back
to three, wearing
her blue Easter dress;

bits of high school prom
mix with honeymoon dust,
her son's third birthday,
and her fourth grade class
where she won a weekly
spelling bee....

She's a puzzle
burned in its box—
five or six pieces survive
that don't match.

Burying the Angel

You sit on a blanket
at Kure Beach, hold
my gift, an angel made
from a spool. You grasp it

in your hands, bury
it in sand, dig it up,
bury it again, a writer
striking the same keys.
You replay your
twelfth year when
you darted between
honeysuckle
into a field, air
brushing hair
into disorder,
your laughter the last
stage of childhood,

before your uncle's
secret sin, his fingers
running up your legs
to the spot that hurt
and hurt until you split

in half, a drama queen
hiding from those hands.

Soon you'll say, *Leave*

me for good, your days
a hand pressed
against a stove eye.

Orpheus Looking Back

He couldn't wait.
The one task Hades asked—
Beauty turned him back—
Eurydice dressed in white,
a bride pulled from death
by beauty of love's desire.

She fades into the passionless
shades, her lover doomed
to join her soon, their deaths

like the ends of all loves,
killed by cares, anger, affairs—
until finally lovers look back
to find Hades's face, patient
as Fate, waiting with open arms.

Old Man in Ephesus, Year 620

I remember the days my father used to carry
me to market on his shoulders. He'd set me
down, and we'd walk hand-in-hand, my sandals
clapping the cobbled street. Many-colored columns
rose so high I thought only God could touch
their tops. The odor of fresh-baked bread mixed
with the sea's scent and fruit from outdoor stands.
Sun bathed he city in yellow light, and the sky,
deep blue, met the blue of the distant harbor.
I laughed, told Father that I wished all this—
he and I together, happy, the city's bustle—
would last forever, but he leaned down and said,
The only thing that lasts is God. I thought
he'd lied, and God, I wish he had.

Those days—when Justinian reigned
in Constantinople, when we thought
our great cities and little joys would last
long past our lifetimes—are as dead as bodies
dumped in common graves, pestilence bulbs
rising from their flesh like rotted fruit.
My father died before I turned twelve,
My mother, too, and my three sisters, their bones
Resting I know not where. The city's still
there, once-great Ephesus, shrunk, it's columns
collapsing like Roman glory, its shops and homes
felled by an earthquake, most markets closed,
and people, starving, begging for food.

What can a man do when the world he's known
is destroyed before he's dead? *The only thing that lasts
is God* my father had said—and now I'm leaving
my family's city to become a monk, to escape
the squalor I know as a man of ninety, nearly blind,
forced to beg. Then I will write about this place
and wonder what a future Herodotus would think
of these troubled times. I suppose that doesn't matter
for me—I only pray that when I die God will guide me
back to Ephesus as it was, where I will feel my father's
strong hands lift me to his shoulders, the odor
of baked bread mixing with the fresh sea-breeze
as we walk inside a city that never ends.

Abelard's Last Letter to Heloise

In your letters to me, my love, you said
you'd rather burn in hell than die without
me. In my lie-filled replies, I claimed
to care for God more, free with advice
extolling you to be a good abbess.

Now I'm old, tired of running from you,
from Bernard's lies about my heresies,
from my lack of manhood at the hands
of Flaubert's men, from knowing I could
no longer please your willing body. Now

near death, I beg you to visit, so I can kiss
your lips to make a pact that when I die,
I'll wait in flames for you to come.
Then we'll join, body and soul,
and make a godless heaven there in hell.

Kidnapper

Don't play too late at night
around an old tree.
When branches turn black
in dying light, you'd better go
inside your house. If you don't,
a branch will pull you up
and hide you in the leaves.
Your mom and dad won't find
you before the tree sucks you
inside its trunk. From there
you'll grow as a branch,
your fingers and toes turning
to leaves that whisper in the breeze.

Pleasant Meal

Chuckles laughs,
licks clown lips,
savors
the flavor
of your flesh.

Snakes in a Pipe

You hear water gurgle down the drain
through pipes to an unseen place—
but you, girls and boys—you know
that snakes live there—two-headed
snakes, deformed snakes with tiny legs
or stumps, snakes with three-inch fangs.
They're born in the sewer, migrate
to pipes, prepare to crawl to your sink,
drawn by the smell of children. So wash
your hands but watch for snakes,
and if you see a head or two
burst through the drain and stare,
beware its bite and go away,
and call your mom or dad to stay
and slay that drainpipe snake.

The Skull

When you're in the store before Halloween,
look at the white plastic skulls gleaming
on the shelves. Pick one up, find a mirror.
Place the skull next to your face. But know
this: that under your thin skin sits something
that grins even when you frown, smiles
when you scowl. Run your fingers down
your jawbone to your chin, up to your lips;

pull them back, get a good look at your teeth.
Imagine your gums gone, your skin flaked
away, your muscles invisible. Examine the remains.
Compare them to your skull. Ponder.

Toy Eater

One morning you'll wake up and find a hole
in your favorite toy and wonder how
it got there—but I will tell you why—
I cast a spell upon a doll who creeps
into your room at night and feeds upon
your toys. She takes a tiny knife and cuts
a hole to pluck and widen at she eats
the toy from inside out—but you're asleep.
It's okay—she leaves before you wake.

Basement Door

You tiptoe to the basement door,
snap off the hook and push
it open. Below you the floor
is covered with dust.
Now you fear to take a step
because you know you'll see a ghost
staring up the steps,
who wants to make you fall
and join its world behind
the dirt-encrusted wall.
Then you'll be a ghost yourself
and you'll try to scare
the boy or girl who opens up
the door that leads nowhere.

June Bug

When the june bugs come out this summer,
you might consider catching one and tying
a string to a back leg and watch it fly around
your head. My advice is *Don't*. I once knew
a boy who made a june bug his toy, but forgot
about there are more than one. His bug escaped,
buzzed its fellow bugs, who flew together
to form a wall. The boy saw them coming
and ran—too late—the bugs caught him,
surrounded him in a whirlwind. His sister
found his skull and a few rib bones. Now if
a june bug flies into your path, it's fine
to pick it up, admire the green gleam of its belly
in sunlight—but be sure to let it go.

Disappearing

As a child I used to watch the minute
hand move on the kitchen clock,
crawling a circle of passing time,
as slowly as December's wait
for Santa. Now years fly by,
and I no longer notice minutes
pass, but stare at the second hand
of my watch, then back to my book
before another look discovers
twenty minutes have passed away.
I pull a calendar out of my pocket,
realize it's Thursday though
I'd thought it was Wednesday.

Today, talking with a colleague,
I said it is 1999, but that was twenty
years ago, which I'd have known if I'd
taken the time to check my face
in a mirror, find the wrinkles that call
to mind Alfred North Whitehead saying
Every moment is perpetually perishing—
I concur, say to myself, *Damn right,
Alfred,* as if I could strike some agreement
with the dead to stretch each moment
like a child pulling silly putty apart.
But time bleeds out of the clock,
which ticks faster as it exsanguinates
until the tick-tock, tick-tock stops.

Child Philosopher

A five-year-old philosopher, I walk
the dirt driveway, past sugar maples,
to the log house, whose white wood siding
gleams in noon light sun. I'm dark
inside because I'm thinking of what
I just overheard—you know how it is,
children just can't keep ears
to themselves. I heard things, strange,
frightening, about a brother I didn't know
I had —Jeffrey, twin. Bad lungs, couldn't
breathe. Died one hour after birth. But I didn't.

I think about death, imagine it, quite literally,
as nothing. Not an empty cup, not the mole holes
I tripped in by the garden, but sheer, absolute
emptiness. Watching TV that evening—
while Mama and Daddy sit at the kitchen table,
arguing about bills—I sit on the slick, freshly waxed
tile floor, see *Davy and Goliath*, claymation Christian,
Easter episode. Fascinated, I watch the moving clay
figures of Davy and his grandmother as they look
at old photos, find a ball and play catch, and talk
the simple talk of child and grandparent. She looks
healthy, vigorous, but the next day, after playing baseball,
Davy returns home and walks into sadness, as his father's
voice intones, *Grandmother died this morning.*

Shocked, I shift on the floor, twist my head away
from the screen, and although I'm only five,

say to myself, *But Davy's grandmother looked fine*
when they were playing in the attic. Now she's dead.
I will die too. When will I die, be nothing, like Jeffrey,
emptiness under dirt? The show over, I run into the kitchen,
which seems stuffed with light, sit in a chair too big
for me, and cry. I hear the clock tick loudly, nestle against
my mother's breast for perhaps the last time, ask
When will I die? When will I die? Mama and Daddy try
to comfort me: *It won't be for a long, long time.*

Later, just before bedtime, I stare at my reflection
in the bathroom mirror, talk to my twin image who stands,
like me, in empty space, and order him to never die.

Daydreaming

A sunny May day outside a third grade
classroom window, nine o'clock.
A boy's mind races to the school bus
coming at two to take him home.
There he'll race with Daddy to a tree
swing chained to a maple branch, fly
across the gravel drive, feet brushing
bushes on the other side. A wall of black
thunderheads boiling in the west interrupts
his daydream. He tries to keep his eyes
on the teacher but can't, hopes she fails
to notice. Darkness shrouds the sky
with a vampire's cloak, and shadows
creep until lightning streaks pierce
dark into unnatural light. The boy
tumbles to a dream where he crawls
on a ledge above a mad scientist's lab.
A skeleton hangs from a hook—the boy
cringes at the sight of machines
and strange light. His eyes open, return
him from dream to school. Hail
and wind beat against windows
and the teacher herds her class
to the room's center. Afraid,
the boy waits for the storm to pass
as children crouch under desks.
The boy feels trapped, nowhere to hide,
no worlds left for his mind to wander.

Old Woman Alone, Reading A Picture of Dorian Gray

Her fingers loosen; the book slips
to the carpet. She starts awake,
scratches her face, flakes of dead
skin falling on her pants. Brushing

them off, she pulls a hand mirror
from her purse and views a sea—
ancient, stormy—of wrinkles
except for the smooth, pink skin
where she'd scratched before.

She takes a razor blade, removes
the rest, head to toe, then admires
her young face, firm breasts, flat
belly, before she falls asleep.
Tomorrow someone will find
her flayed body, bloody skin
curls littering the floor.

Matter

I set my telescope
on a picnic table, aim
for Mars, red in the east.
Moving the scope back
and forth, I try to find
the disk, but fail. My field
of view is full of stars,
lenses drawing them out
of darkness and distance.
I watch them multiply,
spy on them, travel
through light-years
of space and time, see
their past, and know,
concerning me and my
telescope, they don't
give a damn—

Astronomers say
we are made of dust
from stars: carbon, oxygen, iron,
thrown from supernova,
exploding into earth and life
and me. I place my eye
on the scope one last time,
see my own image mirrored,
as if to say *Matter*.

Natural Haunting

Blades of winter wheat cut the cooling sky,
their light green color paling to gray in twilight.
A lone tree guards the field, bony branches ending
in twigs, unclipped fingernails scratching
the young night. Fireflies begin their evening
flights, flashing yellow light, easing growing dark.

Cat paws rustle as the moon rises above the horizon,
illuminating green eyes eager to hunt. Bats
from a distant cave cross the moon and fly closer,
their wings swooshing. A young rabbit scurries,
stopping to eat wheat. As the bats pass by,
cat's eyes move forward, stop, then jump up
and down, disappear. The fate of its prey:
unknown, but a whippoorwill begins its dirge, as if
mourning those who won't survive the night.

Timeless it seems, this natural haunting,
hunter seeking hunted, dance of predator
and prey, everlasting drama of survival.

Hale Woodruff's Georgia Landscape

Green and brown swirls surround
the central darkness. Blades of hay—
living and dead—trees I can't
identify, leaves merged into wind-
blown hair tufts, and bent tree
trunks struggle to live, pulling
themselves from the chasm, striving
to touch the cloud-filled sky.

I want to walk inside the painting,
touch a tree or hay blade, hear
the hum of inward life, wonder
if each leaf and truck is filled with joy
to be alive or afraid of that abyss,
that absence always tugging, never
stopping, sucking life away.

Paradise Lost

My hoe bounces off hard garden soil,
Tennessee red clay dry from lack of rain.
I curse weather reports on TV that claimed
the drought would end last week, as I toil
to turn over ungiving earth, loyal
to the task of growing crops, frustrated as Cain
was by God's rejection—I understand his pain,
his lashing out at Abel, his anger a boil
burning his skin like a mark from God—and yet
I work, the dirt giving a little under constant blows,
wipe sweat off my brow with my t-shirt, fall
down, scrape my knees. I brush them off, get
up, shake my fist at the sun in the east, which glows
like a flaming sword. Dust settles into a red pall.

Empty Grave

Passing the graveyard where my twin lies,
driving on a dirt road at 2 A.M.
on my way home to an empty house, tears in my eyes
from feeling alone, I wonder why I'm

driving down that dirt road at 2 A.M.,
thinking of the half that's six feet under. I'm tired
of feeling alone, wondering why I
care so much about a stillbirth, why I'm mired

in grief, pondering why he's six feet under. I'm tired
of trying to live up to a dead child,
grieving over a stillborn brother. I'm mired
in emotional mud, heart buried under a pile

of pain, driving on a dirt road at 2 A.M.,
passing the graveyard where my brother lies
dead, wood box and cartilage decayed, not a gram
left in the grave where my dead brother lies.

Country Fate

Gazing out my window in late November at a bare oak
losing its last leaves, I walk to the front porch,
sit in an unpainted rocking chair, watch as a bird falls to its death, a fate
sealed by a shotgun blast. I wonder if it was the will of God
that the bird die at this moment, the hunter firing without free will
from a preset path. That's hard thinking for early morning, so I walk to
the house,

hear the screen door slam, the wood floor creak as if the house
has arthritis. Outside, wind blows the branches of the oak
like the legs of a drunken centipede, dry brown leaves clustering on the
porch.
Swirling and swimming in circles, going nowhere, their fate
is to rot, yet I admire the beauty of their dying dance, God
conducting their final flights as if they had the free will

to move. But *I'm different* I think–*I even have freedom
to take a pee when I please*–I hear the noise from the house
buffeted by wind, which carves off loose shingles, rips a limb from the
oak,
flinging it through the gray sky, throwing it to the porch
where it crashes and I startle. *It's not my fate
to die of fear; my old heart's not ready for God*

to take me yet. Once, I believed in a Grandfather God
like my granddaddy who spoiled me and gave me the free will
to do what I wanted. I remember sneaking back into the house
one night after I'd run away. Granddaddy saw me by the oak,
his flashlight shining on my face; walking me to the porch

he cried, said he'd almost died from worry–my fate

seemed good that night—but was it fate,
Granddaddy's mind turned puppet-like by the hand of God,
my will led by the puppeteer to find my way home, free will
as shadowy as the ghost I saw wandering through the house
as a boy, which turned out to be the shadows of the oak
dancing on the floor by the bedroom window, our talk on the porch

an act in someone else's play? I used to dance on that same porch
to Granddaddy's fiddle, moving by means of that same fate
which took him away when I was ten, snatched up by a God
pulling strings–and damn it, I don't even have the free will
to complain; it's as predetermined as the time when this old house
will fall down, as set in time as the falling of the oak,

which with a gust of sudden wind does fall, landing on the porch.
Watching a row of boards break, I accept God's fate,
my lack of free will, feeling invisible strings pull me inside the house.

At the Bell Witch Cave, Adams, Tennessee

Here I sense cold breath
of the last native
American who met death
above this cave from white
man's disease, falling
on the earth, blighted
through time and space
until I, stooping under
limestone roof, see a face
glow with old wrath.

Fear pulls me away,
and I stumble on the path
outside to run on red clay,
safe at last with open eyes
to the one who haunts
and why. The witch rises
from the dust of old sins.

The Moralist

Something whispers in your childhood ear
when your Granny died just yesterday –
a chilly breath as the preacher starts to pray;
you shiver at the creepy voice you hear
that says, *Your fate will be like Granny's, Dear;*
your heart will stop, your breathing halt one day;
your body rot as insects start to play;
your flesh will skeletize within a year.

You'd better be a good child from now on
lest the soul that from your body parts
wanders on its own to emptiness;
but if you're good I'll come to you upon
an unexpected day – you'll never part
from the sleep of blessed nothingness.

Alone in the Dark

Abandoned in the dark he cannot move;
a little boy finds himself alone—
in the dirt-filled basement lights go out.
,

He reaches for the railing on the stairs;
his hands touch only coolness in the air—
in the dark alone he cannot move.

His moth-wing heart rings out rapid beats;
he cries for Mama but she's in the bath—
in the red-clay basement lights winked out.

He senses silent fingers in the gloom
about to grip his neck and start to squeeze—
frightened in the dark he cannot move.
In his mind he sees a skull's death-head;
his feet stick to the ground like solid lead—
in the tomb-like basement lights go out.
From that day he finds himself afraid
of solitary life, detached, apart;
abandoned in the dark he cannot move
since in the dirt-filled basement lights flicked out.

Confidence: An Acrostic

If I'd had time to say goodbye,
Ann, I would remind you of the time
Mary, your little sister, said that when I
Died, I'd be by her side every
Evening, haunting you in the kitchen,
All hell breaking loose when I
Dashed every dish to the hardwood floor.

It worked, back I came, a vengeful ghost,
Angry at your constant criticism of
My writing, denying me the slightest
Inkling of feeling that you cared for me.
Now I whisper in your ear,
Harsh nothings hurting your heart
Every moment of your fear-filled
Life. "Revenge is mine" saith the
Lord – eternal fire is worth the cost

Of your suffering. It's bad enough that you
Live, trying to drain the life out
Of your second husband, ordering him
Round like vulture's screeching.
Damn me, God, for hating
Her, my ex who slept with the neighbor
Each night that I worked
Late. My skin turns to ash as I face the
Penalty of my revenge. But it's all good—
My stay down here, fire making
Embers of my flesh forever damned.

The Problem of Suffering

I watch
my cat,
cancer growing
in his throat.

He tries to eat
but can't
and I know
I'll have him
put to sleep
tomorrow.

Today
he suffers
but can't understand,
can't ask God
Why?

but I can
and do
but the answer's lost
in sad attempts
to chew.

Invitation

A demon whispers in your dying ear,
you know that neighbor down the street who lied,
ruined your life and sent your wife to jail?
Soon you'll have the chance to torture him
and burn his back with torches lit from Hell.
Sense the hatred rising in your soul,
let it fester, grow until it fills
your world with joyful vengeance – get a thrill
from wounding those who hurt you in this life.
Join me, then, in fiery joy of hate,
helping me bring others to this fate.

Tease

You, who breathed life into Adam,
removed his rib to create Eve,
why do you leave me those without
breath, family and friends sickled
by Death, and from You, no trickle

of comfort—only a vague hope
of a land too wonderful to understand—
dead abstractions never helped
a soul lost on a maple leaf ground,
old rotted leavings of life. It feels like

St. John of the Cross's dark night
when World's Light hides in a nest
of kidnapped lives and dead abandoned
eggs. Hope of eternal life lost,
sound of a sickle slicing a silver cord.

Darkness comes, carrying the worst—
death-dreams, screams from an abyss
fading like a train whistle. Sleep, relief,
dawn. You reappear with Morning Light
as your guest. You pull me back, breathe

warmth onto my face and I revive
to drive Despair away until tonight
when You come at two a.m. Then
You touch my shoulder with your hand
and I, awakened, sense You flee again.

Hiding

I used to hide
inside lilac bushes
along a fence line
outside the church
where I worshiped
as a child.

Mama would call me
back and I'd resist,
reluctant to return
to the heat of the sun.

The church was
fundamentalist–God
the Grand Ogre,
his Cyclops eye watching
every move I made.

The preacher once said
that hell was like a stove
burner turned on high–
Put your hand on it
and hold it down,
listen to it sizzle.

I'd cower in fear
on the hard, uncushioned pew,
praying for God to spare
my small soul,

so after the service,
I'd hide, as if
hiding were possible,
as if hope could
keep me straight, safe
from God's fiery glare.

In Hell

If only hell
had flames,
sulfur stench,
demon whips
lashing my bare back—
Time I can't count here,
a place beyond years

but not tears.
Guilt walks
embodied—
my wife's accusing eyes
after my third affair,
my oldest son I struck
for wetting the bed,

the boss I embezzled—
always haunting,
never leaving
since I lack eyes to close,
ears to stop. Again,

again they come,
those I hurt,
nightmares
formed from guilt.

Leave!
I shout

but no one hears—
alone I'm pierced
by accusers' arrows,
knowing they strike
true.

Progress

I was four when our house
burned, a short in a stove wire
turning my first home

into ash. White smoke
rose like hot breath in winter,
fading into a death gasp.

Sometimes I feel myself
fading, steam from a boiling
kettle never reaching

the ceiling. The world, too,
is dimming, a flashlight
with a failing battery,

my heart, a car engine
in cold weather that can't
turn over fast enough. Today,

there's a highway built over
the ashes of my childhood, and I
walk on dust I will become.

The Warmongers' Apocalypse

He feasts on famine,
The Beast, Black Horse,
hollowed death's-head-skull,
mad mouth, heart stuffed
with hate, war, theft, leaving
behind life's losses—the poor,
the beasts, share the same fate—
the rich sleep on peace-softened
beds, unconscious, without
conscience—gates and locks
shelter them from what they
have wrought. But when

the Black Horse leaves, after
the Pale One has its way,
judgment arrives, God's fist
unclenched, tipping comfort
from people who've played
too much with lives, who've paid
for guns, warmongers
and murderers, who will face
pain, death, eternal flame.

About the Author

Michael Potts is the author of the Southern fiction novel, *End of Summer* and the horror novels *Unpardonable Sin* and *Obedience*. He is also the author of an anthology of horror stories, *Death Rattle and Other Dark Tales* and the nonfiction book, *Aerobics for the Mind:: Practical Exercises in Philosophy that Anybody can Do*. He is Professor of Philosophy at Methodist University in Fayetteville, North Carolina. He lives with his wife, Karen, and eight cats in Coats, North Carolina.

Read more at www.michaelpottsauthor.com.

www.ingramcontent.com/pod-product-compliance
Lightning Source LLC
Chambersburg PA
CBHW020351160726
47987CB00022BA/2545